Praise for Traveling Salesman's Son and William Bernhardt's Poetry

"William Bernhardt writes with warmth, wit, and a clear desire to commune with his reader. Whether he is working in free verse or in meter and rhyme, Bernhardt makes of poetry a way of connecting person to person. Like Montaigne, Bernhardt is a man consubstantial with his book, and the full range of human feeling is on display in these poems with great honesty and ardent empathy."

— Benjamin Meyers, Oklahoma Poet Laureate (2014-2015), Crouch-Mathis Professor of Literature, Oklahoma Baptist University (for *Traveling Salesman's Son*)

"In this new collection, Bernhardt comes out guns blazing with the wonderful manifesto 'Get This Over With,' in which, among other things, he tells us to: 'play your bagpipes loud, off-key / skip assignments / let the trash pile up / have ice cream for breakfast'… These poems rove through the minefields of society and culture with the eyes of a seasoned soldier. They roam love's hall of mirrors, knowing when to laugh and when to cry at the distortions. And they take a long thoughtful walk with what it means to be 'family.' It's all here."

— Nathan Brown, Oklahoma Poet Laureate (2013 - 2014) (for *Traveling Salesman's Son*)

"William Bernhardt is one of Oklahoma's and the country's literary treasures....Part William Carlos Williams (the big picture of our national lives) and e.e. cummings (poetry's micro-moments), this new book will bring converts to poetry and to Bill's yeasty vision."

— R.C. DAVIS-UNDIAMO, EXECUTIVE DIRECTOR OF *WORLD LITERATURE TODAY* (FOR *THE OCEAN'S EDGE*)

"You know William Bernhardt as a writer of thrillers, but if you read *The Ocean's Edge*...you will know him as a poet as well—grounded, majestic, hopeful...and funny."

— JACQUELYN MITCHARD, *NEW YORK TIMES*-BESTSELLING AUTHOR OF *THE DEEP END OF THE OCEAN* AND *TWO IF BY SEA*

"Like another lawyer-poet, Wallace Stevens, William Bernhardt writes with force and precision, his diction at once plain and profound. Written in the venerable traditional of American modernism, and sometimes confessional, his lines reveal a man touched by a sense of wonder at everyday experience and the intensity of the commonplace. Clearly, he has come into his own as a poet."

— ALLEN MENDENHALL, MANAGING EDITOR OF *SOUTHERN LITERARY REVIEW*

"Armed with a storyteller's sensibility and his trademark humor, William Bernhardt writes of…longing and loss, irony and humor, the bittersweet complexities of parenting, the secret dreams of writers. His fiction fans will be delighted as William Bernhardt proves himself to be a compelling new voice in American poetry."

— RILLA ASKEW, *KIND OF KIN*, AMERICAN BOOK AWARD-WINNER

"William Bernhardt…combines the novelist's sure instinct for narrative pace and vivid image and ear for the natural rhythms of the spoken word with the poet's sensibility in those telling moments that reveal the soul alive to life. Sometimes with wit and humor as well as pathos, these poems in precise, sometimes startling language draw the astonished reader into shared illumination of the joys and sorrows of existence. Bernhardt the poet—and be assured his is truly a poetic voice—deserves attentive reading, and his poems quickly earn our admiration."

— CARL SENNHENN, OKLAHOMA POET LAUREATE (2001-2002)

Traveling Salesman's Son

Traveling Salesman's Son

William Bernhardt

Copyright © 2022 by William Bernhardt

All rights reserved.

No part of this book may be reproduced in any form or by any electronic or mechanical means, including information storage and retrieval systems, without written permission from the author, except for the use of brief quotations in a book review.

For my father

Perhaps the world will end at the kitchen table, while we are laughing and crying, eating of the last sweet bite.

— Joy Harjo, "Perhaps the World Ends Here," *The Woman Who Fell From the Sky*

Part One

Get This Over With

You wouldn't read poetry
unless you're seeking happiness
so let's cover that upfront

You want to be happy?
To laugh, cry, fly,
       find freedom?

Kill your gods
Every one of them
silence those nattering voices

defund the cranial police
spit out the wafer
get off your knees

play your bagpipes loud, off-key
skip assignments
let the trash pile up
have ice cream for breakfast

fill your house with cats
read late into the night
question authority
use sacred texts for kindling

form your own choir
sing a hymn to yourself
left-swipe lessons time forgot
fairy tales contrived to pacify peasants

Celebrate the dawn of the New Genesis
cultivate your own garden

where knowledge is the sweetest fruit

build your cathedral plank by plank
worship regularly
bathe in your power and glory

forever
Amen

Daddy's Little Girl

There's no explaining
        how some people burrow into you
        earthworms of the heart
except that sounds so unpleasant
and you have never brought anything
        but pleasure
        since the day you were born.

Perhaps there is explaining
        how you've burrowed into my heart
        since we are both so much
the same. But I don't feel that way
looking in the mirror, only
        when I look at you,
        the silver lining of my life.

Explain this:
        I know you must go
        I know you must grow up
move on. You can't be Daddy's girl forever
except—you are, and will
        be, like it or not, my reminder
        that life is good, sometimes.

Helplessness

a woman in tears
sits on a bench in the quad
she's lost her job
lost her love
her reason for getting up

is everything okay?
can I help?
stupid stupid stupid
well-meaning but useless
empathy and Kleenex

drunken busker
abducted teen
unappreciated artist
failed father
brain-damaged slob
never stood a chance

like shells buried in sand
crashing waves scatter the driftwood
I am unable

Traveling Salesman's Son

He's home again
at least for a while
delivering Commandments
from Suburbia
which we will ignore
he won't be around to enforce them

How long this time?
Sundays are torture
but soon the workweek will resume
his anger will dissipate
he'll fall asleep mid-sentence
and we will count the days

He prefers life on the road
the pleasure of satisfied customers
the prestige of position
he's a success
he's moving product

Home is less a triumph
patronizing to her
brutal to us
because that's the way it's supposed to be
why don't we understand he's right
why don't we understand he's in control
employees are more compliant

Only when the road grew short
could we see the cracks
revealed by flashpoints of violence
the deal he could never close
was the only one that mattered

It Talked Back to Me

Plastic, gray, big as a boot box
I carried that first clunky tape recorder
everywhere. Bought to record my sister's
performance, but I was the only one who could
make it work. Tinny monoaural microphones
snaking like tentacles, sucking up the
sounds of my childhood, detachable speakers
clipped to the base, jittering
like timpani through tinfoil.

That tape recorder was my best friend. I
recorded my favorite songs, stitched together
with pretentious commentary, a clueless DJ
tossing words in the magnetic void. I listened
as did my chores, I huddled with it
beneath the bedclothes. It talked back
and let me pretend someone was
listening. My lifeline, my earliest pathway.
Out.

The recorder finally failed and I buried
it as you might a member of the family,
with due reverence and awe. Sometimes,
late at night, when no one watches
I still hear those songs and dance.

The Other Poet

The peasant shirt or the bow tie?
Faded jeans or tattered? Loafers? Sneakers?

I should be alone with my pen
but who can resist the adulation

twelve people in a church basement
waiting to hear my art

What are the new
emerging forms? What do you think

of modern poetry? (I try not to ha ha)
Are today's poets too difficult?

Only at the bar. I started scribbling
sometimes it's hard to remember why

the competition is fierce
because the rewards are miniscule.

Some nights I lie in bed, staring
at the ceiling, seeing stars

I want to climb to the top of the
mountain and scream

But tonight, here, with my apostles,
the elite twelve

there is solace
I am poet, critic, comedian, cultural

clairvoyant. They need never know
the tie is a clip-on.

Inferno

I've been dead before
so I can write with authority
didn't care for it much
too much noise, everyone talking at once
the television always on
the radio tuned to the same station
too much drinking
perhaps they had to
no one could see the sky.

None of the metaphors work
Death is a cocktail party
Death is a three-day binge
Death is knowing you've disappointed your children
Death is your wife in that stiff-backed chair
Death is disappointment
lies that come unbidden
judges you've never met
And all the things you don't know.

Time Travel is More Complicated

When they were young, I read to my children
every night, first together then separately
as their tastes and reading levels diverged.

My Father's Dragon, Charlie and his chocolate.
Anne of Green Gables.
If I could freeze time, preserve

a single moment in amber, it would be that.
If I could fly faster than the speed of light
it would be to travel there

that bedroom, children clustered, listening
from the fourth dimension
Last night, Alice said, Hey Dad, wanna hear

something funny? She read it to me
just as I once read to her. I closed
my eyes and listened

laughter making my eyes water.
Time travel is more complicated than I realized.
But then, so is everything.

Gap Year

College students take a gap year
        But I took one too
They do it because they need more time
        I did it because of you.

Did you think that you destroyed me?
        I'm afraid that you did not
Damaged, yes, and broken then—
        Now you're an afterthought.

You wanted so to cause me pain
        To twist the sharpened knife
But the lasting pain is just your own
        The impact's on your life.

Your face looks pale; your gait is weak
        The years have done you wrong
I took my lumps and forged ahead
        That gap year left me strong.

You want to hear I pine for you
        Sorry, incorrect
You had your chance, you turned it down
        It will not resurrect.

Of course I'm thinking of you now
        But here's the truth, cupcake
This poem's not a laurel branch
        No, stupid girl—a stake.

Telos

He searched for meaning all his days
        the purpose-driven life
        the zealot's enthusiasm.
First he found it in his parents
        but they proved fallible
        he needed Higher Authority.
He turned to religion
        the reassuring fable, diminished
        by multi-faceted flavors.
Secular love seemed certain, intense,
        fleeting, marred by
        agenda conflict and angst.
Politics seemed surer
        but ardent logic and credibility
        yielded to approbation and pathos.
History became his truth
        hard evidence, fact
        shrouded by the recorder.
Science was his new faith
        but the clarity of reproducible results
        could not fill the lacunae.
Language could, it defines us
        there's always a word for it
        shared experiences never experienced.
Not till the end did he come
        to poetry. The quest for a
        single perfect image. He did not
        find it, but for once, there was
        solace in the imperfection.

The Birthday Balloon

see the string
bobbing
gentle restraint
velvet handcuffs
cages at the zoo

but for that string
it would disappear
as would I

Ash

I had the dream again
the one that ends with screaming
our whole crew was there
and you, shadows slashing your face
we were so young
we knew nothing about sex
we knew nothing about drugs
we didn't know death would take you first

I dream in black and white
chiaroscuro horror
blood dripping from your eyes
chocolate tears
the shrill siren split the night
and fog descended like a choking leather vice
choking

I dream you almost every night
shut out the light and there you are
fireflies beneath my eyelids
I can't go back
except
when Morpheus brings
his realm of ashes
let my eyes always be open

Christmas Eve

The shank of December, our reindeer return
From college and colleagues, conch shells
From an increasingly distant shore.
We pretend snow has fallen.
But heat rises with each fallen footstep
May midnight bring us peace, not pieces.
I hold my breath, darkness dissipates.
Hope is the star shining overhead
leading our wise ones back, once more.
We are merry.

Loss

hurts, until
you get used to it
as indeed we all must

I had this house, only one
I ever loved
whirlwinds of fortune

we were close there
had a city I loved, gone
a car I loved, gone

vicissitudes of fortune
had a cat, gone
a caretaker, I

shouldn't've trusted
had this naked doll
and you, of course

you get used to it
you have no choice
change is inevitable

appointments in Samarra
the measure is how one deals
so I deal

you can learn this too
get used to it
don't feel so much

face it, no one else

really cares
pathetic wretch, wrapped

up in his own losses
till he can no longer see
the horizon

there is no solace
don't feel so much

the smile is a shield

Refugee Camp

      The cocoon does not comfort
           the firewall's a farce
insulation, not solace, not warmth
      The chrysalis has shattered
           miasma intrudes
with chatter, agenda, and truth.

      We are all exiles, he says,
           you know it's true,
of that sort, or this, or another
      We want to fit in
           or do we, at that—
isolation, not solace, not warmth

      The snow is a shroud
           the blanket a bust
too little, too loathing, too late
      My hand is outstretched
           you cannot see
we are all exiles.

Sestina Ceasura

The sestina as a form permits repetition
convenient for poets with a dearth of ideas
each end-word must be chosen carefully
as it will recur many times. Maddening
and yet there may be solace in old forms
like old socks, old songs, old dachshunds.

So here we go: begin the repetition
each end word must be chosen carefully
a poetic challenge the reader may find maddening.
What is the purpose of these old forms?
A poem breathes not wordplay but ideas.
Why did I choose "dachshunds?"

Is anything worth dying for? Are we carefully
recompleting standard forms?
The body aging, brain slowly maddening
each day less innovation, more repetition.
A soul destroyed by bad ideas.
And now we come back round to "dachshunds."

Sometimes there is comfort in repetition
Old wine rebottled in new forms
Snuggle close, you can be my dachshund.

Dusk

The streets are dimly lit
glow from the corner lamppost
      barely seeping through
trash, vermin, human waste
the buildings in ruins
when I close my eyes
sometimes
that's all there is to see.

It's too easy to vent
hide beneath a shroud of pain
surely there is something more
if we let it find us.

Poetry is defiance
an ear trumpet in a vacuum
a megaphone for the voiceless
and a wry riposte
      to the outstretched arms of death.

On the Road with Emily

It's not that her vision was too small
        but her experience too limited
she wanted for fresh horizons
        so I decided to take Miss Emily

on a road trip. She sits shotgun—
        never having learned to drive.
We'll let Google Maps navigate
        so we can focus on other matters

like the transcendence of the soul
        the ephemerality of experience, and
whether pan pizza is superior to flat crust.
        We see the sights. I realize

that I'm thirsty, but she only wants
        a liquor never brewed. We keep the Sabbath
with Taylor Swift for a chorister, and we freak
        when we hear a fly buzz. I'm not

stopping, I inform her, not for Death
        not for Immortality, and not for
clean restrooms and pecan divinity, 17 mi. ahead.
        We finally make it

to the beach, though she tells me
        she was hoping for Disneyland.
She dips her toes into the Pacific—
        and the Wren's eyes

are electrified. She sheds the white dress
        and dons capris. She joins
the women's volleyball team and surfs.

    She sunbathes topless.

As we leave the beach long past dusk
    She takes my hand and tells me
now she knows what it means to be a Belle
    but not one word of her poetry will change.

Insubstantial Pageant

When legend becomes fact,
Stewart tells us, you print
the legend. But what if
there is no legend and
no one remembers the facts?

I hated that sketch, so I
erased the lines, redrew
them, and never satisfied,
did it again, until the original
image had completely disappeared.

There are things only I know
saw, felt, experienced, and
even if I share with someone
vaguely attentive, it won't
mean the same. It's gone.

Did we make our mark? Did
we alter lives, will we be
read, or at least fondly
recalled, when the embers
cease to smolder, and the
hearth holds only ash?

October Chill

We never really connected
though I've known you longer than anyone

distance—something missing
a relationship in passive voice

Disappointment on both ends
never paved a smooth road

Who dug this bottomless ravine?
Never tell anyone

child, parent, partner
they're not what you wanted

Evermore

Though we all wish for some form of immortality
perhaps we would be better off without

A freshman wrote
"*The Ocean's Edge* fails

to fulfill the slender promise
of its predecessor, *The White Bird*."

Now he must elaborate. "The closer the poet comes
to honesty, the more elusive the poetry,"

or, "Here he retaliates against
a string of women who jilted him."

"The preoccupation with sex is rather embarrassing."
True or false, doesn't matter.

Write and write and write.
Stumble across something transcendent

and perhaps, be your own validation
Read the words to yourself

now and again, as the windows
of your garret fill with snow.

REB 2017

So today you're off again
when I start down memory's sieve
I see less of my path
and more of yours
I recall your first day
augurs of the momentous
smart, independent, resilient
creating your own games
writing your own stories
I never did enough
because so little was needed
you let me hug you today
a sop to the doting dad
but you left the security of that embrace
and soared, beyond my grasp
to the other side

Memos

Memo to Myself, Ten Years Ago

You are about to make the most titanic mistake
I would tell you not to do it
but I am unclear whether history can be rewritten
outside the realm of memory. I don't mean
to scare you, but your life is about to become
so bleak, so loveless, so unsure.
You will wander lost, and the few with
outstretched hands
are not there to help you up.
You will find a way out, but you will never
recover.

Memo to Myself, Five Years Ago

Bad news. You are about to make the most titanic mistake
even worse than the other one.
This is the one you will never
forgive yourself for. Inhale deeply,
because when you realize what you've done
you won't be able to breathe, entombed
in a barren mountain of ice
you will hide
you will crawl, and eventually
you will find your way out, but the cost
will be unbearable.

Memo to Myself, One Year Ago

Has it taken so long
to learn the truth? And isn't it sad
that you can only stop

the hamster wheel from spinning when
there are so few days left to spin? This mistake
may not be your worst, but it's the one
you will never escape. No way out.
Could you find a way in?
A new resolve,
an intermittent flash of serenity?

Memo to Myself, Today

Now you understand what matters
you had to lose it
first. But surprise—today you make
the most titanic mistake of your entire life.

Inauguration Day

Never let it be said
    that we did not see the beast approaching
Never let it be claimed
    we were fooled
Never let us pretend
    we did not know what we were doing
    we did know
    and still we followed

Never let it be thought
    we could not hear the brutish footfall
Never let it be imagined
    we were not to blame
Never let us shrink
    or hide, evade, deny
    it was no one else's fault
    only our own

Someday it may be said
    the cataclysm made us stronger
Someday it may be claimed
    we emerged the wiser, but
Never let us pretend
    that this was meant or had to be
    was inevitable as dying
    this is the world we deserve

Sisyphus

when I feel myself trembling
backward
into the twilit abyss
you catch me
that's what partners do
but when you stumble
always the same twilight
always the same abyss
you won't be caught
you won't relinquish
the void you must return to
even though it is killing you

Enquiries

Could anything be sadder than
an empty swing blowing in a breeze?

Is silence made of peace
or loneliness?

Can you say you know me if
you've never seen me bleed?

Do you hear the ocean speaking
when you are lost at land?

Does the flower smell of honey
or the other way around?

Subtext

Kaitlyn the Amazon Warrior
Caitlyn, Assassin for the Cult of the Red Scimitars
Kaitlin Who Must Be Obeyed, and
Katelyn, Princess of the Lost Continent
will never know
how I keep them distinct
or how I amuse myself
as I discuss the evils of passive voice
they are unaware
I am not merely their teacher
but Sir William, Professor
of the Seven Secret Signs,
last practitioner of shimbitzu—the
deadliest of martial arts—and
Hallowed Knight of the Sacred Students.

Twyla

The baseball cap can never hide you enough,
pulled down low, brim almost touching

your chin, bulging backpack brandished
like a shield. I can barely see you.

The classroom isn't large enough
for you to sit as far back as you would like.

What secrets are concealed
by a monochromatic wardrobe?

Is that faraway look turned outward
or inward? Do you gaze into the future

or the past? And what of the present?
This moment. Now. If.

Your strength could be towering.
We are who we wish to be.

Exposed

It was bound to happen
How long could I go on fooling?

So now you know.
Feel better?

Maybe two steps back
Is a step forward

on another field
where cool pastels beckon, a moment

before the horse-drawn jailor
brings a housewarming gift

Alias

Why do we start the day
    by looking into the mirror
somehow contemplating
    who will emerge
who will strap on shoes and face
    the grimoire, while the other
remains in the looking-glass
    looking

Why have we fallen so far afield
    from feeling, it hurts
the pain like a bit drill
    to the gut, any release
is welcome, the unforgiving
    don't feel it, they remain
in the looking-glass
    looking

When tomorrow comes perhaps
    he will be the one who promenades
down the boardwalk, tipping his hat
    and smiling without the eyes
When will we learn that all
    we have is caring, keeping
    choosing
    looking

Part Two

Jeopardy!

Clues
200 Fire
400 Youth
600 Life
800 Peace
1000 Regret

Correct Responses
What is the soul?
What is glass?
What is a nanosecond?
What is elusive?
What is the heaviest element?

oklahoma twilight

behind the brittle sunset
the shimmering truth:
forest given to plowshares
red dirt
        crowning
                all that remains

fragrance creates dissonance
silvered wheat, more man
than nature
the whippoorwill wind
        reminding
                that which remains

shall we plant a garden
as others did before
use without possession
the tallgrass teases
        beckoning
                hold fast, hold

Traveling Salesman's Son Laments

Ken dolls have no fingerprints
and of course, no genitalia
but damn, they dress well
hair just right
handsome smile
some are even doctors
and they all have the big house and
trophy Barbie
everyone envies

That is what you wanted
you pushed so hard
that many were snared
by that plastic mold
where all that is undetectable
is what lies behind the smile

I failed you
but I kept my fingerprints

Troll

loser
has-been
drunk
silly ass
why do they get all the breaks?

i have all the luck
both kinds
the system is rigged
money talks
i should be running this joint.

i have a voice
they cannot silence
i'll post and post and
anonymously
i will be heard.

i know more than they think
i am not a cipher, not invisible
i stare at the screen
lurking but
alive, i exist, and
i will prove it.

Mythos

someone stood on the turret
saw how far the fall
knew how high the sky
and wanted a piece
      —less so, she
           the combined weight
                was unsustainable

Icarus soared
crashed
hubris, scholars said—
or inevitable
the price of flight
impalement
      gravity is fate
           rising above
                standing   out

only he can see
the wind his only woman
sailing toward the silvered sunset

Handmaids

we are still children
barely out of the cradle
running too soon

our own worst enemy
working against our own
      interests

cannot see beyond the fog
cannot see beyond the words
we cannot taste   truth

we cannot feel
          what lies
     the surface
          beneath

Physics for Innocents

If there are parallel universes
born each time a choice is made,
whim spinning into infinity,
then I want an interdimensional subway transfer:

It is always spring
we live by the beach
everyone has everything
children happiest of all

builders free to build
artists to create
no one fights for freedom
it is given gladly

no vice, no vitriol, no zoos, no zeros
merit, not money
we all care for one another
and yet, even here

you are no longer with me
which says so much
       goodbye

The Great Commission

literature is a sacrament
take the cup
drink deeply
dilate your mind's eye

decades ago
I wrote a story
about a boy star-gazing
centuries ago
which you read
today
we shared the moment
holy trinity
you saw what he saw and I saw
you were not alone

do this in remembrance
of what we have yet to share

Do You Know Why I'm Smiling?

Do you know why I'm smiling?
This thing I am—made up
        in isolation, no compass
no one showed me
the way
I invented all of it
        on the bridge between stardust and dirt
and then reinvented and reinvented
is it any wonder
I got a few parts wrong
bumbles, bobbles, brouhahas
but not one second wasted
and every single thing that sought to kill me
didn't
I made this thing I am
and you can too.

1966

In the suburbs
even the conformists
wanted something different
they gathered to share

alternate spellings of girls' names
man jewelry
fake hair—a suffusion of
bridge candy

tall metal percolators
coffee cake
pop culture jibber jabber
you're never home because

love what you've done with this room
aspiration desperation dust
the pungent warfare
of disparate perfumes

if I behave myself
an endless ocean
separating what we wanted
untenable, but providentially
so much room for rebellion

Incantata

The spring is made of minefields,
      but you can come to me
The valleys stretch forever
      the black exceeds the blue
They do not love you as they should
      treachery abounds

Seas of tears and tyrants
      but you can come to me
Jealous gods, petty pawns
      the noise exceeds the song
You will survive, though not alone
      for you can come to me

Full of Sleep

For quite some time I loved you so
        and I did foolish things
mind-altering you, this
intoxicant
        see what devotion brings?

The brain fights back, reasserts,
        eventually succeeds
the stupor fades
what have I done?
        the sober body bleeds.

I've recovered, yes, but now dwell
        within an enemy camp
did you care
or simply need?
        I'm getting writer's cramp.

Smile

My mother always smiles
she chooses to be kind
      because others had not been
and happy
      because it was so hard
      being around those who aren't
she wouldn't increase the pain
      there was already enough
But I need that pain
      want it
      that pain defines me
it's why I'm here
So you will have to forgive me:
I will not be smiling
      today.

Guilt

I should've said something
instead the memory haunts me
an endless replay
what I should have said
to one so superior

fear is the prison
silence is the sentence

say again

you mumble
when I say I love you
translation:
I won't be blamed

hold on

i know you believe you will never
        get over this but
you are strong

we know complaints are
        wasted words, we know
life is a broken promise

i wish i had an incantation
        to wish this all away
        pages blank
so fill them

the story has no climax

everything hurts
everything heals
hold on

Story Structure

Boy finds a bird
the bird knows the way
water shapes soil
river rounds curves
ocean brings life
knowledge skips stones

Girl finds a rose
the rose knows the way
sun shapes petals
shadow shapes stems
forest brings life
love climbs trees

Boy finds a girl
knowledge finds love
one eye watches
one eye sleeps
gods do not create earth
we create gods

Birthday Letter

What have I done?
Bringing you to such a place
dominated by savagery, brutality.
Winter oozes
crude poison, and somehow
you survive.

My heart aches
there is no anodyne.
I could not save
myself and I cannot save you.
I cannot pretend I wish you
gone, but your eyes haunt

me, my home is eternal
but this changes nothing, pain
is your true inheritance, yet
you must survive.

draw me into darkness

as I was drawn from it
smallest seed in the cosmos
pulsing starstuff, inexplicable
purposeless

silent lilies in the graveyard
bitter breakfast of winter
the polyethylene park
I bow before

the budding amaryllis on
my tabletop
pulsing, promising—
purpose found

Part Three

Here I Plant

pluck the dried husk
turn the soil, water, repeat

Here I order the shelves
organize, systematize, repeat

Here I decorate and dance
and play and sing and put

pencil to paper, erase, repeat
I will stay here

the scarecrow in the garage
policing the accumulation

of years and dust.
You don't need to see it—

Here I am surrounded by light
though I am all of darkness

Here I am engulfed in noise
though my center is silence

Here is constant motion
though I am heavy with thought

Here is laughter and life—
a cultivated cathedral.

Abyss

Can you forgive me
for what you know I've done?
we never speak of it

    never
but it is always there, when we are together
    when I am alone

I have never loved anyone
so much or so well
I will not see this kind of love again

better to lose an eye
than lose your gaze
as I have

I journeyed from the safe shore
to the ocean's edge
thinking myself invulnerable

failing, flawed, feeble
rebuilding on foreign soil
not everything can be recovered

This is a requiem
I will never stop trying
and failing

the bald man with the cane
distant eyes, age and pain
seeking undeserved grace

Can you forgive me
For what you know I've done
And what you don't and what I haven't?

Swee'pea

Forgive me if I failed
    to notice that my source of
    perpetual sunshine
found herself in shadow.

I had to emerge
    from arrogance and twilight
    from guilt and aggravation
to see you in the sun.

You soar with each day's dawning
    you are the gentle guide
    the wisdom of our children's tongues
We come to truth from love

Violence

Could you stop fondling your gun
long enough to notice that our
children are dying?

No, it isn't pornography, it isn't
Ritalin, it isn't television or
video games or bad parenting, unless

parents put the bump stocks in
their kids' hands
Mental illness will always be

with us, the silent serpent
lurking in the glade—guns
optional.

Is ego more important
than children? Your need to exercise dominance?
Your campaign contribution?

We will not make America greater
until we realize that everything
that kills children kills us
first.

Exasperation

well of course I could survive without you
would it make you happier
    if I couldn't?
of course I will die alone
    we all will

open your eyes
change, or accept that nothing will
    change
I am too full of miracles
    to be dragged down by your rubbish

Regret

you picked me up and hurled me
so far from myself
took me years to
crawl
back

now here you are again
so far from myself
and I find I cannot stop you
any more than the wheat
can stop the scythe

the hero's journey

the hero's journey
searching for a miracle
never realizing
the journey is the miracle

Revival

If you say a prayer
to the mirrored glass

bow and scrape
and kneel and fast

If the crosses aim
like daggered stakes

and the feast turns in
to wine and cake

I slam the brakes and seize the snakes
though the host of angels pity

And if at last
the luncheon crowd

proclaim the Word
much too loud

the fevered brow becomes ashamed
as they burn the books of pleasure

The Ringleader

I just wanted to remind you
that I am important
smartest guy in the room
I can make jokes no one laughs at
I can play morality cop and music critic
from my exalted perch

I was not Daddy's favorite
doesn't matter
some teachers were impressed
not other kids
not girls
doesn't matter
I will reduce them
to a bundle of body parts
they would be lucky to get near me
but no one ever gets near me

frat house three-ring circus
I was
happy, finally, mostly
they understood that I was somebody
if not somebody they liked much
doesn't matter
rich white overlord
except I was never rich enough
never white enough
never in command

My wife doesn't listen, or like it, or love
doesn't matter
Do you know how much $$$ I've made?
What does that tell you?

The boys moved on
doesn't matter
Got my own world
looking out for number one

And when at last the bad news comes
Who cries?
doesn't matter
I'm the ringleader
What happened to my circus?

Ivy

You surrender
everything
because you cannot bear to be alone
You wear the blindfold
      blocking out the light
You close your lips
      and let her sew them shut
You shed your clothes
      and stand there in your shame
You shed your skin
      so you can feel
      everything
between the sheets you find the ivy
      twine your legs in leaves
      rooted in dirt and dust
In the end, you find that perfect moment
      of pleasure, or pain
and in the shimmering afterglow
You see the faces of billions
      who have gone before you
      or are with you now
and for that hallucinatory moment
You are not alone

David

David strums his lyre
to entertain the troops
he sets their minds on fire
he conquers fleeting groups

The audience is thinning
like hair upon his head
but he can tell he's winning
with each new face in bed

Those partners never last
he can't help but wonder why
bad luck, bad choice, bad bombast
he's the monarch butterfly

He strums again and presto
he's stronger than before
taller, slimmer, faster
he's found the song once more

Abstinance

At dinner you reminded everyone
that God loves you
because you're doing it right
but late in the evening
after the sugar rush of two desserts faded
I saw the crack
behind that smug smile
the hope of resurrection
not strong enough to suppress
the emptiness of evidence
or the perpetual skepticism
of the human mind

Stereotypes

You marry for advantage
to make the hollow whole
And you will always leave the men
whom you cannot control

And all the sexist stereotypes
that you insist are true
Are not about the men, I fear
they're only true of you

Social Distancing

The couple making love
        on the other side of a thin motel wall

The showmancers plotting
        on the other side of a screen

The people in the pages of a romance
        or the lyrics of a song

You were admitted
        to my private place
        my closed room
        narrow bed, against
        the long cold night

The true circle of life
        is reaching out
        driven by loneliness

And now we're told
        to stay six feet apart

Must I come so close?

Part Four

The Reason Asian Restaurants Disappoint

is, let's face it, the fortune cookie
which isn't even Asian, it's from San
Francisco, home of clanging cars and
lobster bisque, not prognostication—
but I digress.

These vague forecasts, worse than horoscopes,
are lost opportunities
diners expecting so much and receiving
so little, generalities about
tall dark strangers and prosperity
around the corner. If I get a bad one
she smiles. If I get a good one she says
"You already have everything," which might
suggest a flaw, not with the cookie, but
the dining companion.

Just once I'd like to crack open the cookie,
unfold the paper, and read:

> *That stock you bought last week? Sell. In fact,*
> *sell everything and move to Cabo, where the sun*
> *shines every day and the cost of living is*
> *affordable, even for a writer.*

When I'm feeling low, what
wondrous change might be wrought by:

> *Tomorrow at noon, at that veggie burger joint*
> *you like, you'll meet a woman who will*
> *quicken your heart, broaden your mind*
> *and also makes an excellent mushroom tortellini.*

I've returned today for lunch, consuming the cookie before the meal, hoping to find:

> *Here is the plot of the book that will make you a trillionaire.*

accompanied by a detailed sixty-chapter outline.

But instead, as I unfold that scrap of paper, breath suspended, pulse pounding, I find:

> *Good work is its own reward.*

The waitress does not understand why I want a refund.

The Game of Life: Rules

no pink and blue pegs
no cute convertibles
no random paths

spin the wheel
1-4
settle
5-8
earn a degree, then settle
9-10
add a new path
that isn't on the board
can't be pegged

Next turn
1-4
blame
5-8
project
9-10
accept and ignore

Choose one:
clone
victim
renegade

whether you stay on the board
or make your own
all players end on the same space
not Millionaire Acres
not the Poor House

the shadowy space
we cannot see clearly
until we land there

Finding Peace

I tell stories for a living
I make music for myself
my Class 2 narcotics
stories, games, music, puzzles
the only time I leave my head
completely absorbed

I craft a song from rudimentary scores
or my ear, devising an approach
to make it work, strategizing
vocals with fragile tools
an act of creation
as all my narcotics are

no pretense
I won't be playing Carnegie Hall
I hear the slamming doors
the snarky whispers
none of which matters
This for me

when it goes well
it's impossible not to feel it
inspiration, executed
stories, games, music, puzzles
joy raises the roof
transcendental teleporters
conduits to parallel universes
no dystopias, no
disembodied brains in jars
no mortgage, no marriage
no gossip, no grief

the salvation of a chord
the transmigration of the spirit
a few precious moments of peace

Traveling Salesman's Son at Play

I was usually alone, as a child
but loved to play board games
so
I would invent opponents, usually
named for celebs on TV game shows
I played both contestants
yet still generated a surprising
degree of strategy and surprise
so
from the very start, you see, I
was living an unsustainable schizophrenia.

In time, I became the emcee
and my imaginary gladiators played
the game independently, or so it
seemed, in the battleground of my brain.

Is it any wonder that I can entertain
multiple characters in my head and
they argue and fight and love and kill
as I put their lives on paper?

I'm still usually alone, but the world
has invented games that can be played solo
so
I've set my imaginary playmates free.

I hope they will live good healthy lives
but I worry about them
on their own for the first time
Bob and Abby and Pat
IRL the world is so much harder
than a game show—

actually, that's what IRL is
on a larger scale.

I will leave the door ajar, my friends
perhaps we will reunite for the endgame
when playmates are hard to find
and the rules no longer matter

Stardate 2.10461

I have encountered a quantum disturbance
in this new cosmic life, I'm
a man of action, not words
a bold explorer
new worlds, new frontiers
battling for universal truths

but sometimes late at night
as night is measured here
I see the distant light
I peer beyond it to that other life
and wonder which is better
or even if they are different

Ghost Lover

I took a ghost to bed with me
        and thought myself discreet
I shed my clothes too eagerly
        but she retained her sheet.

What then ensued I won't describe
        I fear you'd be amused
You choose a ghost, you must expect
        the horror that ensues.

Bustopher and Me

Snow brings comfort
as all blankets do—

So today we will walk,
my cat and I, his one
      white whisker blending
      into the background

As I stomp in my hiking boots
making snow angels with my foot
his head darts to one side
What did he see?
a flitting bird
a resilient insect
I prefer to believe he has
seen a snow nymph, a creature
that exists only on the periphery of
feline vision

Humans will always miss her
but those yellow cat eyes
see more profoundly not only
      in the dark of night
      but the dead of winter

At last we return home
stomp the snow off my boots—
his are forever white—
pour a cup of coffee
settle beneath another blanket
and write something
while the cat settles in my lap

Our snowy adventure reminds
there is a larger world outside
though for ourselves
we prefer the world we've created

The Writing Process

I am flummoxed when questioners
ask me to describe
my writing day
what could possibly be more tedious?

My cat wakes me at 5 a.m.
I feed him, start the coffee
water my plants, activate the aromatizer
exercise my impinged arm
take deep breaths
grab a blanket, settle into my recliner
and create new myths
for a world in need of them.

Fascinating, huh?
At some point, I'll have breakfast
a soft-boiled egg and toast.
Later my cat will curl up beside me.
That's pretty much it
unless UPS brings a package
or some other world-shattering event occurs

So my advice to writers?
Well, you need a cat, obviously.
Adopt a rescue kitty, there are many
and the blanket is essential
--beyond that?

Close your eyes, wiggle your fingers
make *your* myths
explain this world we're trapped in
to minds that cannot

or prefer not
to see the proper path

Give us a better reality
You can do this.
Just wiggle your fingers.

Skiing Taos

The furious wind bellowed across
the mountaintop, trying to push us
off its sacred summit, plummeting
into the charcoal sky.

It does not want us here

And yet we remain, perched
precariously atop two
tongue depressors pointed like geese
in formation, bracing against the
bitter cold

We have risen only to descend

The towering aspens form a perimeter
the hawks are hall monitors, and
the occasional dollops of risk
remind us that nothing lasts
especially that which you cherish most

We are here because you wished it

And even if I might prefer
a padded chair and a good book
by the blazing fire back at the lodge
This is majestic

I have rarely seen you so elated
so infused with the joy that is surely
why we have come
the only possible purpose
for all that we encounter

when we leave the mountain

Surgery

When I had my tonsils removed
age eight
they gave me ice cream
When I had my appendix removed
age twenty-eight
it felt like a paid vacation
no suits and ties just
lounging and loved ones
all day to read, three square meals
and ice cream.

But the hernia repair and the kidney stones
age you-don't-need-to-know
were different
I recovered at home, where the trash
still needed to be emptied, the email
monitored, and something must
be prepared for dinner

But the real difference
is Time's winged Tesla, the
anesthesiologist reminding you that
this could be the time
you fall asleep and don't awaken.
Have I done enough?
Have I provided for the children?
Who will feed my cat?

Even the most vigorous
routine cannot prevent the
glass from clouding. If
mortality defines us, what words are
writ in the devil's dictionary

beside my name?
The paper is brittle and the mirror
crack'd, and all we remember are
good times, good books, good people
and peace

Ralph

Joy!
Unbridled joy!
As we whisk down the mountain
drive down the road
challenge uncharted routes for the
      last of us, the two of us
joy, so hard to find
so infrequent a guest
but always welcome.

Congratulations.
You've compensated
for the sleep-deprived nights
the dirty diapers
the projectile vomiting
the impossibility of finding shoes
      that fit—
debt paid in full!

In fact, I'm the debtor now
you never asked to be born but
I came begging
I have no means to pay this debt
but I will never stop trying.

Words

There's a war raging overseas
        glaciers melting
        another school shooting
so many we hardly notice anymore

I sit in my recliner
        scribbling poetry, but
my own life is not without trauma
earlier I couldn't find
        my favorite writing pen
        I'm out of coffee filters
        and my cat gave me a love-nip
            that hurt

I'm not delivering world peace
        capturing carbon
        quelling disputes—
unless

words matter

what would the world look like
if instead of being raised on
        toxic masculinity
        conspicuous consumption
        competitive religion
we were raised on
        Dickinson
        and Frost and Collins
        liquors never brewed
        roads not taken and
        Whale Day not Veterans Day

and we explained ourselves with words
composed on brown recliners

Empathy is the magnetic north of literature.

How to Murder a Rooster

It shouldn't be that hard to figure out.
I am a professional crime writer, after all
    so I have the credentials
I see this more as a cozy mystery
    than a hardboiled one
    it doesn't involve a head of state
    nor the crown jewels
just one thoughtless, insistent, slumber-shattering rooster
    who starts crowing at 3 a.m.
    and never stops

It's not like I live on a farm
    this is a neighborhood, with paved driveways
    and recycling trucks, and a fake pond
the neighborhood association fined us when
    my son parked his car in the street
but our backyard neighbor can keep a rooster?

The direct approach is usually best
    but snipers are hard to find
    I don't own a gun
and it would be obvious a murder had occurred

Bludgeoning with a blunt instrument
    seems too violent
    though I believe I could've brought it off
    at 3 a.m. this morning

Poisoning is subtler
    and unless an autopsy is performed
    probably undetectable
    The Scourge of Sleep would be eradicated

In my mind I picture a weeping family
> two parents, a dog, a little girl in pigtails
> holding a small ceremony with candles
> and a shoebox for the deceased

I offer feigned condolences
> then race to the block party
> where I'm high-fived by everyone else
> in the neighborhood

Abduction is another option, as are
exsanguination, defenestration
drawing-and-quartering
but it's important to maintain perspective

What if I were caught?
Would there be a trial?
Would I be castigated for animal cruelty
> or given a tickertape parade?
> Perhaps a small award in honor of
> services performed
> for the betterment of mankind

I can see the headlines
FOWL PLAY IN FOREST GLEN
> a Twitterstorm erupts
> cancel culture sidelines me
> my books go out of print
> I end up a bum on a street corner
with a weathered cardboard sign
ANYTHING HELPS
until a police officer kicks me in the shins
and tells me to move along

Or maybe I'm tossed into the slammer
Convict No. 24601

the storied jailbird who killed a bird
    Would the other hardened cons scorn me
    for silencing nature's boombox?
I feel as if I've lived an entire alternate life
    the rise and fall
    without lifting my head from the pillow
I wonder if there could be a second act
    a comeback
    but that seems extremely complicated
during the dark terrible moments
of a sleepless 3 a.m.

Funereal Thoughts

Parents Are Required to Have Many Awkward
      talks with their children, mostly
      puberty-related
      but
The Worst by Far
      is the talk about what to do
      when I'm dead or dying, so here it is:
      if I'm brain-dead, forget it, and
      if you're not sure, give me the
New York Times Monday crossword
      if I can't do it, pull the plug, but
      that leads to the problem of how to treat
      my remains, should I be buried or
      cremated, personally
I Want to Be Exploded
      people look up and see a red blur
      in the sky and think, "There goes Bill!"
      or perhaps, "Even in death, so needy,"
      if you're hesitant, let me remind you
Cremation Comes with Problems
      what to do with the ashes
      an urn on someone's mantle
      or they could be
      scattered, but you must
Pick A Place
      and please do not scatter me at Disney World
      or Broadway or the library, I mean, so obvious
      I'd rather be at home
      but you know how I hate a messy house so
Maybe This Could Be the Ultimate Prank
      ashes siphoned into someone's gas tank, or
      sprinkled on toast like cinnamon for
      someone you don't like

>   at this point you may be thinking
> A Family Plot Seems Simplest
>   but remember to leave room for
>   all of us, and my cat, who assures
>   me that I won't
>   be in charge of this
> One Way or The Other
>   so better not to worry about it
>   just cuddle up and
>   take a long nap

Traveling Salesman's Son Wields Words

I'm in my sixties now
but they still tell the story
of the Christmas party where Little Billy
    four years old at the time
stood on the fireplace seat
in a red nightshirt
and recited A Visit from St. Nicholas
without error

Another favorite—Billy
age five carrying his father's
How to Beat the Stock Market
and
reading passages aloud.
"That kid is going somewhere."

Nah. That kid loved words, books
and there were few age-appropriate
    in the house
so I read what was there
even my much-older-sisters' tattered
Nancy Drews, until my father
informed me they were Girl Books
not that I cared
but I think he was worried about something
my father called fiction
"stories for girls"
movies, too
real books contained factual information
why waste time
with something unprofitable?

Later at the library

I found The Hardy Boys
and The Three Investigators
substitute sleuths of the proper gender
and my favorite, Encyclopedia Brown
puzzles! mystery! fictional Sudoku
must I explain the appeal?
a brainy kid on a bike
with a tough female pal to ward off
        the bullies.

When no one was watching
I read Harriet the Spy
and its scandalous sequel
and soon started keeping a notebook
        of my own snotty observations
        about those around me
until a chance remark suggested
my mother had read it
that ended my career as a spy

My favorites were comic books
smuggled into the house
if my father found them he would
crush them in his huge hands
apoplectic, angry, shaking
Funny books are for morons!
So of course today I have thousands

and hundreds and thousands of words
millions, trillions
pirouetting around me every day
asking if they can have the next dance

My life is blessed many times over
but the happiest part of every day
is late afternoon, a quiet place

a comfortable chair, and a book
girl books and boy books
because those stories
are all true, and they
never insult, only challenge
they wrap me in their ink-stained arms
and show me how to live

Memory Worms

Tunes get stuck in your head
a TV jingle
a melody half-heard overhead while
I stood in queue for a cashier
like sticking a pacifier in my mouth
But now I'm plagued by memory worms
random pieces of the past
that resurface, unbidden
more important incidents disappear
but not the time my father scolded me
in a crowded room
the time she and her clan waltzed past me
as if I were invisible
my dumbstruck silence in the presence of the Master
occasionally a happy recollection arises
the debate tournament joke that landed
the Christmas Eve you brought the best stocking ever
but what my hippocampus refuses to relinquish
is humiliation, disappointment, sorrow, regret
given the multitude of choices
this selection process seems perverse
like sifting the wheat from the chaff
and keeping the chaff

Message? Freud might say
      unfinished business
      unresolved angst
      teaching moments left unlearned
or maybe the subconscious has a better sense
      of the truly remarkable
which is not winning a big award
or hitting a bestseller list
but smaller moments when truth falls short

Since we cannot declare a mulligan in real life
we replay the moments in our minds
until at last we have rewritten experience
more to our liking
which may be a way of learning
or just sticking a pacifier in our brains
as we queue up for the final checkout line

Leavetaking

the distance in the evening
the whispers in the kitchen
when you did not want to plant flowers
in the spring
i knew you would not be here
in the autumn

Traveling Salesman Bids Farewell

the wise wag once remarked
that no one on their deathbed

ever wished they'd spent more time
at the office

but there are exceptions
he sits alone at his desk

lap covered with junk mail
trying to find relevance

another year passes
mote in the maelstrom

family life bored him
he loved acclaim

all those insecurities retreat
into the folds of a tan coat

prejudice is insecurity
insecurity is fear

college can't cure that
if your eyes are on the wrong prize

in the mist I see echoes of
an alternate path

less money, less success
more time for the rest

leading to a different place
and a different end

some comforts
don't come in the mail

Final Tweet

This is my twitter to the world
that seldom spammed to me

two-hundred-eighty characters
of needless chatter

the story not altogether mine
Let me acknowledge the obvious

parents, spouses, children, thanks for allowing me
time to write, as if you had any choice

And thanks to the teachers who shaped this
positronic brain, led me to this story

not altogether mine
And thanks to the gossips, backstabbers, insecure

jealous, greedy, solipsistic liars
tweeters, tweakers, twiddly twerps

who helped me see more clearly
I have loved every one of you, and still do.

About the Author

William Bernhardt is the author of over sixty books, including two other collections of poetry, *The White Bird* and *The Ocean's Edge*. He has received the Southern Writers Guild's Gold Medal Award, the Royden B. Davis Distinguished Author Award and the H. Louise Cobb Distinguished Author Award, which is given "in recognition of an outstanding body of work that has profoundly influenced the way in which we understand ourselves and American society at large." In 2019, he received the Arrell Gibson Lifetime Achievement Award from the Oklahoma Center for the Book.

www.ingramcontent.com/pod-product-compliance
Lightning Source LLC
Chambersburg PA
CBHW032003060526
44107CB00158B/1326/J